W9-CFQ-875

Kids' Travel Guide

Washington, DC

FlyingKids presents:

Kids' Travel Guide
Washington, DC

Author: Kelsey Fox, Shiela H. Leon

Editor: Carma Graber

Designer: Slavisa Zivkovic

Cover design: Francesca Guido

Illustrations: Slavisa Zivkovic, Francesca Guido

Published by FlyingKids Limited

Visit us @ www.theflyingkids.com

Contact us: leonardo@theflyingkids.com

ISBN 978-1-910994-39-9

Copyright © 2018 Shira Halperin and FlyingKids Limited

All rights reserved. No part of this publication may be reproduced, stored in retrieval systems, or transmitted by any means, including electronic, mechanical, photocopying, or otherwise, without prior written permission of the publisher and copyright holder.

Although the authors and FlyingKids have taken all reasonable care in preparing this book, we make no warranty about the accuracy or completeness of its content and, to the maximum extent permitted, disclaim all liability arising from its use.

Acknowledgments:

All images are from Shutterstock or public domain except those mentioned below:
Attribution: 22mb-By The White House, White House Photography Office; 29mt-RadioFan at English Wikipedia, CC BY-SA 3.0; 29mb-By Mariordo (Mario Roberto Duran Ortiz) (Own work), CC BY-SA 3.0.

Key: t=top; b=bottom; l=left; r=right; c=center; m=main image; bg=background

Table of Contents

This is the only page for parents in this book ...

Dear Parents,

If you bought this book, you're probably planning a family trip with your kids. You are spending a lot of time and money in the hopes that this family vacation will be pleasant and fun. Of course, you would like your children to get to know the city you are visiting—a little of its geography, local history, important sites, culture, customs, and more. And you hope they will always remember the trip as a very special experience.

The reality is often quite different. Parents find themselves frustrated as they struggle to convince their kids to join a tour or visit a landmark, while the kids just want to stay in and watch TV. Or the kids are glued to their mobile devices and don't pay much attention to the new sights and places of interest. Many parents are disappointed when they return home and discover that their **kids don't remember** much about the trip and the new things they learned.

That's exactly why the **Kids' Travel Guide series** was created. With the Kids' Travel Guides, young children become researchers and active participants in the trip. During the vacation, kids will read relevant facts about the city you are visiting. The Kids' Travel Guides include puzzles, tasks to complete, useful tips, and other recommendations along the way. The kids will meet Leonardo—their tour guide. Leonardo encourages them to experiment, explore, and be more involved in the family's activities—as well as to learn new information and make memories throughout the trip. In addition, kids are encouraged to document and write about their experiences during the trip, so that when you return home, they will have a memoir that will be fun to look at and reread again and again.

The Kids' Travel Guides support children as they get ready for the trip, visit new places, learn new things, and finally, return home.

The *Kids' Travel Guide — Washington, DC,* focuses on America's capital. In it, children will find background information on Washington, DC, and its special attractions. The *Kids' Travel Guide — Washington, DC,* concentrates on more than 14 central sites that are recommended for children. At each of these sites, interesting facts, action items, and quizzes await your kids. You, the parents, are invited to participate or to find an available bench and relax while you enjoy your active children.

If you are traveling to Washington, DC, you may also want to get the *Kids' Travel Guide — USA*. It focuses on the country of the United States—its geography, history, unique culture, traditions, and more—using the fun and interesting style of the Kids' Travel Guide series.

Have a great Family Trip!

Hi, Kids!

Flag of Washington, DC.

If you are reading this book, it means you are lucky—you are going to Washington, DC!

You may have noticed that your parents are getting ready for the journey. They have bought travel guides, looked for information on the Internet, and printed pages of information. They are talking to friends and people who have already visited Washington, DC, in order to learn about it and know what to do, where to go, and when ... But this is not just another guidebook for your parents.

This book is for you only—the young traveler.

So what is this book all about?

First and foremost, meet Leonardo, your very own personal guide on this trip. Leonardo has visited many places around the world. (Guess how he got there ☺?) He will be with you throughout the book and the trip. Leonardo will tell you all about the places you will visit ... It is always good to learn a little about the city you are visiting and its history beforehand. Leonardo will give you many ideas, quizzes, tips, and other surprises. He will accompany you while you are packing and leaving home. He will stay in the hotel with you (don't worry—it doesn't cost more money)! And he will see the sights with you until you return home.

Have Fun!

A travel Diary—the beginning!
Going to Washington, DC

How did you get to Washington, DC?

By plane ✈ / train 🚆 / car 🚗 / other _____

Date of arrival _MONDUMC 0 TH_ Time _2:00PM_

Date of departure _SUN AUGES 5TH_

All in all, we will stay in Washington, DC, for _____ days.

Is this your first visit?   **Yes No**

Where will you sleep?
In a hotel / in a campsite / in an apartment / other _____

What sites are you planning to visit?

_____

_____

_____

What special activities are you planning to do?

_____

_____

Are you excited about the trip?

This is an excitement indicator. Ask your family members how excited they are (from "not at all" up to "very, very much"), and mark each of their answers on the indicator. Leonardo has already marked the level of his excitement ...

very, very much

not at all

Leonardo

6

Who is traveling?

PASTE A PICTURE OF YOUR FAMILY.

Write down the names of the family members traveling with you and their answers to the questions.

Name: _____

Age: _____

Has he or she visited Washington, DC, before? yes / no

What is the most exciting thing about your upcoming trip?

_____

_____

Name: _____

Age: _____

Has he or she visited Washington, DC, before? yes / no

What is the most exciting thing about your upcoming trip?

_____

_____

Name: _____

Age: _____

Has he or she visited Washington, DC, before? yes / no

What is the most exciting thing about your upcoming trip?

_____

_____

Name: _____

Age: _____

Has he or she visited Washington, DC, before? yes / no

What is the most exciting thing about your upcoming trip?

_____

_____

Name: _____

Age: _____

Has he or she visited Washington, DC, before? yes / no

What is the most exciting thing about your upcoming trip?

_____

_____

Preparations at home
DO NOT FORGET…!

Mom or Dad will take care of packing clothes (how many pairs of pants, which comb to take …). So Leonardo will only tell you about the stuff he thinks you may want to bring along to Washington, DC.

Here's the Packing List Leonardo made for you. You can check off each item as you pack it:

☆ *Kids' Travel Guide — Washington, DC*—of course!

☆ Comfortable walking shoes

☆ A raincoat (One that folds up is best—sometimes it rains without warning …)

☆ A hat (and sunglasses, if you want)

☆ Pens and pencils

☆ Crayons and markers (It is always nice to color and paint.)

☆ A notebook or writing pad (You can use it for games or writing, or to draw or doodle in when you're bored …)

☆ A book to read

☆ Your smartphone/tablet or camera

☆ _____

☆ _____

Pack your things in a small bag (or backpack). You may also want to take these things:

☆ Snacks, fruit, candy, and chewing gum. If you are flying, it can help a lot during takeoff and landing, when there's pressure in your ears 😮.

☆ Some games you can play while sitting down: electronic games, booklets of crossword puzzles, connect-the-numbers, etc.

 Now let's see if you can find 12 items you should take on a trip in this word search puzzle:

Leonardo
walking shoes
hat
raincoat
crayons
book
✓ pencil
camera
snacks
fruit
patience
good mood

P	A	T	I	E	N	C	E	A	W	F	G
E	L	R	T	S	G	Y	J	W	A	T	O
Q	E	Y	U	Y	K	Z	K	M	L	W	O
H	O	S	N	A	S	N	Y	S	K	G	D
A	N	R	Z	C	P	E	N	C	I	L	M
C	A	M	E	R	A	A	W	G	N	E	O
R	R	A	I	N	C	O	A	T	G	Q	D
Y	D	S	G	I	R	K	Z	K	S	H	D
S	O	A	C	O	A	E	T	K	H	A	T
F	R	U	I	T	Y	Q	O	V	O	D	A
B	O	O	K	F	O	H	Z	K	E	R	T
T	K	Z	K	A	N	S	I	E	S	Y	U
O	V	I	E	S	S	N	A	C	K	S	P

Washington, DC— America's capital

Washington, DC, is the capital of the United States of America.

Because it's the capital of all 50 states, it is located in a district—not a state. The "DC" stands for District of Columbia. Washington, DC, sits on the East Coast of the United States—right between the North and the South.

Help Leonardo find Washington, DC, on the map of the United States.

Quizzes! Which states border Washington, DC? Look at the map if you need help.

1. _____

2. _____

ANSWER
Maryland and Virginia

Washington, DC, is often simply called "DC"—short for "District of Columbia." The name Columbia comes from Christopher Columbus.

Does your state or country have a nickname?

What is it? _____

A few more things about Washington, DC ...

Motto: "Justia Omnibus," which is Latin for "Justice for All."

What is **the motto of** your state or country?

_____

Song: "The Star-Spangled Banner," which is also the national anthem **of the** United States.

What is **the song of** your state or country?

_____

Washington, DC, Here We Come!

You'll especially enjoy the city if you love to eat! People from all over the world live and work in Washington, DC. They brought traditional foods and customs from their home countries with them. In fact, many of them have opened restaurants to share their food with others. During your trip to DC, pay special attention to all the different types of foods you see and try.

What does Washington, DC, Look like?

The spot for the US capital had to be carefully chosen so that it was neither in the North of the country nor in the South. Washington, DC, was not a big city when it was chosen as the capital. In fact, there was hardly anything here at all. But as the United States and its government grew, so did Washington, DC. Government agencies, businesses, and people all flocked to the capital. Today, Washington, DC, is a large city that creeps into two different states. The different sections of the city are called **neighborhoods**.

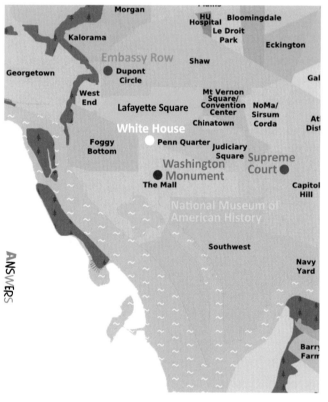

Washington Monument is at The Mall; the Supreme Court is on Capitol Hill; the White House is in Lafayette Square; Embassy Row is in Dupont Circle; the National Museum of American History is at the Mall.

ANSWERS

In Which Neighborhood Are These Sites Located?

Look at the different neighborhoods (their names are in black type on the map). Can you figure out in which neighborhoods these sites are located?

Washington Monument
_____

Supreme Court
_____

White House
_____

Embassy Row
_____

National Museum of American History
_____

Where I'm Staying
_____

Did you know?
The oldest part of the city is Georgetown. It was established in 1751. That was 40 years before Washington, DC, was officially founded!

Washington, DC—how it became a great capital!

Deciding where to put the capital was not easy for the founding fathers. Alexander Hamilton and the northern states wanted the capital to be in the North. But Thomas Jefferson and others wanted to make sure it would be in a place that was friendly to the southern states. George Washington, the first US president, got them to agree on a spot along the Potomac and Anacostia Rivers.

The US Constitution made Washington, DC, the country's capital in 1790. Since then, it has been **the heart of America's government and power**.

What is the name of the capital of your state or country?

Today, DC is a great city with people from all over the world. But there's one problem with living in DC. Because it isn't a state, its citizens can't elect representatives to Congress. They can choose a delegate, but the delegate isn't allowed to vote. Only the representatives from the 50 states can vote to decide US laws. In fact, up until 1964, the people of Washington, DC, weren't even allowed to vote for President 😞.

Did you know?
During the American Civil War, bread for the soldiers to eat was baked in ovens on the grounds of the White House. Both the Civil War and the War of 1812 were hard on Washington, DC. In both wars, parts of the city—including the Capitol Building and the White House—were harmed.

Getting around DC

There are many exciting ways to get around in DC that may be different from how you travel at home.

Check the box for each kind of transportation you tried while visiting!

☐ **Walking**

Many of DC's most famous sites are within walking distance of one another—so a lot of people choose to walk, hurrying from one place to the next.

☐ **Taxi**

Washington, DC, taxis can take you quickly from one part of the city to another.

☐ **Metro**

To feel a little more like a native, consider hopping on the Metro. This underground train stops near most of the city's major attractions. Most people who work in DC take the Metro to get to work—so the trains can get pretty busy during rush hours.

Exploring the National Mall

Put on your walking shoes! The National Mall is considered **America's Front Yard.** Leonardo wants you to know that many of the best things to see in DC are right here. The Mall is a beautiful, tree-lined boulevard that goes between the US Capitol and the Washington Monument.

Did you know?
Every year, nearly 25 million people from all over the world visit the National Mall.

Cherry Blossom Festival

Seventy percent of the trees on the Mall are cherry trees—a gift to the US from Japan. The date for the **Cherry Blossom Festival** is based on when the trees are expected to bloom each spring. Crowds from all over the world come to the beautiful festival!

Look at the map below and mark the places you visit.

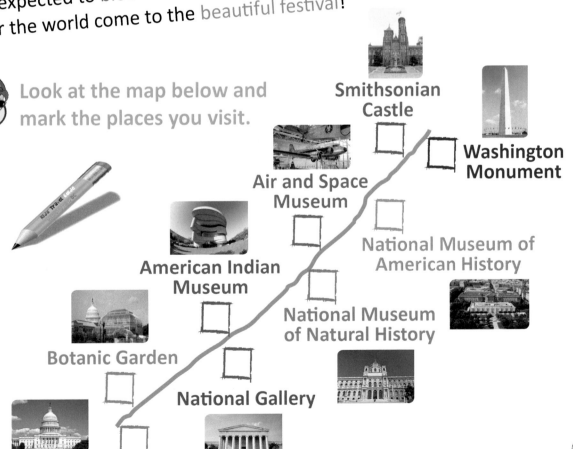

Smithsonian Castle

Washington Monument

Air and Space Museum

National Museum of American History

American Indian Museum

National Museum of Natural History

Botanic Garden

National Gallery

US Capitol

Magnificent monuments and memorials

You may have already seen the towering **Washington Monument**, or heard about the **Lincoln Memorial**, but did you know there are important monuments all along the National Mall? These monuments and memorials are beautiful pieces of art. They **honor** the important men and women who helped make the United States what it is today.

☐ Washington Monument

You're not likely to miss this tall monument to America's first president. To find out more about the monument, including a list of fun facts, see page 19.

☐ Lincoln Memorial

You can learn more about the Lincoln Memorial on page 18!

IN THIS TEMPLE
AS IN THE HEARTS OF THE PEOPLE
FOR WHOM HE SAVED THE UNION
THE MEMORY OF ABRAHAM LINCOLN
IS ENSHRINED FOREVER

☐ Vietnam Veterans Memorial

This touching memorial was built to honor the members of the American military who were **killed** during the Vietnam War.

Did you know?

As president, Lincoln was the commander in chief of the Union troops (the North) during the Civil War. But some people say the back of his head on the Lincoln Memorial was sculpted to look like Robert E. Lee, the general for the Confederacy (the South). What do you think?

Even more great monuments ...

Korean War Veterans Memorial

This powerful memorial has 19 statues of soldiers—all a little taller than an actual person. The soldiers show the different races that make up America. They were made to look like a squad on patrol.

National World War II Memorial

This large monument **honors** the many American soldiers who lost their lives fighting **World War II.** It's one of the Mall's newer memorials. It has 56 pillars, one for each US state and territory that the soldiers came from.

Thomas Jefferson Memorial

A 19-foot-tall (5.8-meter) statue of Thomas Jefferson stands in the middle of the dome at this beautiful memorial. Besides being America's third president, Thomas Jefferson was also the first US Secretary of State and the author of the Declaration of Independence!

Martin Luther King Jr. Memorial

In the 1960s, Dr. Martin Luther King Jr. led a peaceful "**March on Washington.**" Thousands of people flocked to the National Mall to show their support for **Civil Rights for black Americans.**

Tip! Leonardo says that if you have time, visit the Korean War Veterans Memorial during the day and again at night. When it's dark, the statues begin to look like ghosts!

Leonardo wants to know which monument was your favorite. Why?

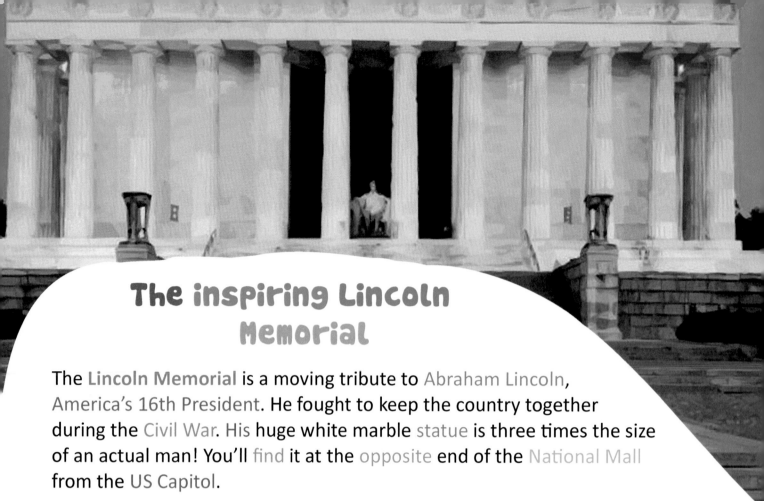

The inspiring Lincoln Memorial

The **Lincoln Memorial** is a moving tribute to Abraham Lincoln, America's 16th President. He fought to keep the country together during the Civil War. His huge white marble statue is three times the size of an actual man! You'll find it at the opposite end of the National Mall from the US Capitol.

Abraham Lincoln was **born in a log cabin to a** very poor family. He worked **hard to** educate himself—and even taught himself to be a lawyer!

How much **do you know about** Mr. Lincoln?

Kentucky; a beard; the Emancipation Proclamation

ANSWERS

☆ Abraham Lincoln lived in Illinois. But in which **state was he born?**

☆ What was "Honest Abe" known for wearing? (Hint: **It's not his stovepipe hat!**)

☆ Which of Lincoln's famous speeches secured the freedom of slaves in the United States?

 Help Leonardo find the Gettysburg Address that's printed on the Memorial's south wall. Can you read what it says? This short speech—272 words—is one of the most important in American history!

Tip!

The Lincoln Memorial looks especially beautiful at night when it's lit up.

IN THIS TEMPLE
AS IN THE HEARTS OF THE PEOPLE
FOR WHOM HE SAVED THE UNION
THE MEMORY OF ABRAHAM LINCOLN
IS ENSHRINED FOREVER

Great Views from the Washington Monument

You've probably already noticed this towering monument to America's first president, George Washington. But did you know that it was once the tallest structure in the world? Or that it is made of stones from all 50 states?

Leonardo has five fun facts to tell you about the Washington Monument!

1. When the Monument was completed in **1884**, it stood **555 feet high** (or about **169 meters**). It was the tallest man-made structure in the world—until the **Eiffel Tower** was built in **1889**.

2. You can see over **30 miles** (or about **48 kilometers**) from the top of the monument!

3. A special trowel (a small tool) was used to lay the cornerstone of the Washington Monument. It was special because it was the very same trowel that George Washington used to lay the cornerstone of the **Capitol in 1793**.

4. There are **193 memorial stones** lining the inside of the monument. These stones were gifts from the 50 states and many foreign governments

5. There are **50 American flags** surrounding the monument—one for each of the US states.

Tip!

Leonardo loves to see DC from the Washington Monument! For the best view of the city, take the elevator to the top of the monument. But don't delay! Tickets are free, but there are only a certain number available each day. So get to the monument early and join the line.

The National Gallery— awesome art!

The National Gallery is one of the most popular museums in the United States. It was given to the people of America by a man named Andrew W. Mellon. He was an art collector from Pittsburgh, Pennsylvania, and he wanted the United States to have a national art museum that was as beautiful as the ones in other countries. So he offered to build a magnificent building, and to put his large art collection there !

Soon, other American art collectors began giving their own collections to the museum. Today, the National Gallery is home to thousands of paintings, photographs, sculptures, and more.

Some of the world's most famous pieces of artwork belong to the National Gallery.

Can you find these special works of art in the gallery and label them with their titles?

1)

2)

3)

4)

5)

6)

Leonardo wants to know which one is your favorite:

ANSWERS

1) Young Girl Reading; 2) Little Dancer Aged Fourteen; 3) The Japanese Footbridge; 4) The Railway; 5) Woman Holding a Balance; 6) Self-Portrait

An artistic alphabet

Complete the alphabet with the names of artists, paintings, and sculptures you find in the National Gallery. Leonardo has already filled in a couple to get you started.

A _____

B _____

C _____

D _____

E _____

F _____

G _____

H _____

I _____

J _____

K "Knight's Heritage"

L _____

M _____

N _____

O Osias Beert the Elder

P _____

Q _____

R _____

S _____

T _____

U _____

V _____

W _____

X _____

Y _____

Z _____

Did you know?

Every piece of artwork in the National Gallery has been donated by generous art collectors.

Tip! Be sure to use the artist's first and last name.

The White House— home of the First Family

The **White House** is one of the most famous houses in the world. Its address, **1600 Pennsylvania Avenue**, is well-known to Americans. The US President and the president's family (and pets!) live at the White House. It also houses the president's office, called the **Oval Office**. Some of the country's most important business takes place here. The White House is located between the Washington Monument and the Lincoln Memorial.

☆ The White House has 6 levels, 132 rooms, 35 bathrooms, 412 doors, 147 windows, 28 fireplaces, 8 staircases, and 3 elevators. How would you like to live in a house like that!?

☆ Before 1901, the White House was known as the "President's Palace" or the "Executive Mansion." President Theodore Roosevelt gave it the name "White House."

☆ The White House kitchen can make dinner for as many as 140 guests!

The Red Room

We visited the White House on

_____

Did you know?

It takes almost 600 gallons of paint to cover the outside of the White House 😮!

We think the White House **is**

☐ Magnificent 😮

☐ White 😏

☐ Not Impressive 🙂

Special holidays at
the White House

For most of the year, the White House is a place of important business—the president signs bills into law, meets with government officials, and entertains members of foreign governments (just to name a few things)! But on holidays, the White House becomes just like any other house—full of decorations, parties, games, and fun—but maybe with a little more security 😊!

Christmas

Christmas starts when the live tree is delivered to the White House by a horse and wagon. Volunteers spend hours decorating the tree in the Blue Room of the White House. Other parts of the White House are also decorated, and an even bigger tree is decorated on the South Lawn! The pastry chef makes a giant gingerbread house, holiday cards are made for the troops, and local choirs and school groups **sing** Christmas carols for the First Family. Around this same time, a menorah is lit to celebrate the eight nights of Hanukkah.

Easter

Easter is a lot of fun at the White House. For over 135 years, the White House and First Family have held the Easter Egg Roll—with live music, basketball and tennis, the Easter Bunny, and of course, **Easter Egg Rolling!** Each year, nearly 30,000 people gather on the South Lawn of the White House for this exciting day!

Did you know?

If you want to take a tour of the White House, your parents will have to make the arrangements at least three months in advance!

Do you celebrate Christmas? yes / no

If yes, do you have special preparations for Christmas?

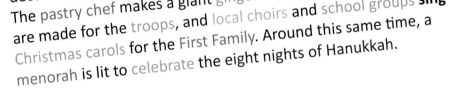

The Smithsonian— so much to explore ...

The Smithsonian Institution is the world's largest museum and research center! In fact, it's actually **19 different museums in one spot**—along with the National Zoo, and nine research areas 😗.

But there's a little bit of a mystery in its beginnings ... An English scientist who had never once been to America provided the money to build it. In fact, **James Smithson** had never met any Americans. But when he died in 1829, he left all his money to the United States.

He said his fortune should be used to build a "Smithsonian Institution" in Washington, DC. In his will, Smithson said he wanted the institution to increase and spread knowledge.

To this day, no one knows exactly why he left all his money to build a big museum in America ... but it was a wonderful gift 🙂!

Leonardo has been traveling all around the world, and suddenly he has forgotten which museums are part of the Smithsonian and which ones aren't ... **Try to help him**—check only the museums that are part of the Smithsonian:

☐ National Museum of Natural History

☐ Botanic Garden ☐ Far East National Gallery

☐ National Gallery of Jewelry ☐ National Gallery

☐ American Indian Museum

☐ Air and Space Museum

☐ National Museum of American History

☐ National Museum of Toys and Games

☐ Louvre Museum

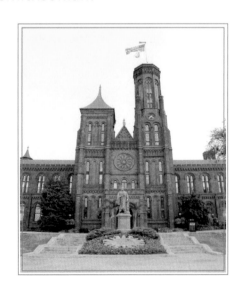

All of these museums are located on the National Mall.

ANSWER

Quizzes!

What do all the Smithsonian museums above have in common? If you are not sure, you can get a BIG hint on page 15.

ANSWERS

The museums that are not in the Smithsonian are the Louvre Museum, Far East National Gallery, National Museum of Toys and Games, National Gallery of Jewelry.

24

Fun things to do at the Smithsonian

There are many exciting things for you and your family to try at the Smithsonian:

- ☐ Do an art project
- ☐ Ride on the Carousel
- ☐ Zoom through the universe at the Planetarium
- ☐ See a live show at Discovery Theater
- ☐ Watch a movie at the IMAX Theater's three-story-high screen

  and much, much more ...

The Smithsonian is one of Leonardo's favorite places to go. He always has fun there and learns new things.

Which museums are you and your family planning to visit?

_____

_____

Which museum are you most excited to see?

_____

Did you know?

The headquarters for the Smithsonian is nicknamed "The Castle." Can you see why it got this name ☺?

Did you know?

Two of the museums even have special sleepovers for kids and parents!

TAKE A PICTURE OF THE MOST BEAUTIFUL MUSEUM BUILDING YOU SAW.

The wonders of the National Museum of Natural History!

Welcome to the National Museum of National History!

Look at dinosaur fossils, see rare colored diamonds and gems, watch tarantula feedings at the Insect Zoo, and much, much more!

The Smithsonian National Museum of Natural History is one of the most important museums and research centers in the world 😮.

Here are some of the exhibits Leonardo wants to make sure you see on your trip:

☐ **Museum Grounds: Urban Bird Habitat**

The museum has created habitats for the many birds that live in the DC area. Birds can come to these areas for food, water, shelter, and a place to nest. Walk through these peaceful places and see how many birds you can spot!

Did you know?

This huge museum is the size of 18 American football fields!

☐ **Dinosaur Fossils**

Perhaps the most famous exhibit of the entire museum is the hall of dinosaur fossils! Wander through the hall and marvel at the size of these prehistoric creatures.

Can you make a list of all the dinosaurs you saw?

The Hope Diamond in the Harry Winston Gallery

Would you like to see **the world's most famous piece of jewelry**? The Hope Diamond is on display right here! Here are some of the astonishing reasons why it's so famous:

◇ Many people believe the diamond is cursed because bad things happened to some of its owners! What do you think?

◇ King Louis XIV of France bought the Hope Diamond in 1668. But after Louis and Marie Antoinette had to leave France during the French Revolution, it was stolen. It didn't turn up again until 1812 in London.

◇ Despite its extreme value, the Hope Diamond was mailed to the Smithsonian in a plain brown paper wrapper!

What exhibits would you add to Leonardo's list? _____

Write a postcard to a friend and tell him or her about your favorite part of the Museum of Natural History!

My dear friends,

_____

_____

_____

_____

_____

_____

_____

_____

National Museum of American History— fun things from America's past

A 1964 Ford Mustang, the set from a 1970s TV show, the beautiful gowns worn by the First Ladies ... If you want to learn more about the United States, its history, and its pop culture, there is no better place to go than the **Smithsonian National Museum of American History**. For years, the museum has collected some of the most important American artifacts.* Each of the museum's exhibits will take you into an important time or place in US history.

*artifact: something made by humans that has historical importance

Oh, Say Can You See!

The most famous exhibit at the museum is the **Star- Spangled Banner.** You'll be surrounded by the battle that inspired Francis Scott Key to write his famous poem—which then became America's national anthem.

The flag you'll see is almost 200 years old and 30 x 34 feet (about 9 x 10.5 meters) in size 😮! You'll learn all about its history—and what the flag and the song have meant to Americans through the years.

What was your favorite piece in the National Museum of American History?

_____

_____

_____

The **American History Museum** is full of one-of-a-kind pieces from history.

Leonardo can't remember where he saw some of the things below. Can you help him by drawing a line between each artifact and its museum exhibit?

Then check the boxes of the things you saw on your visit.

☐ The first car driven across the United States

☐ George Washington's **uniform**

☑ Dorothy's **ruby** red slippers

☐ Covered **wagon**

☐ Mary Lincoln's dress

☐ Greensboro lunch counter

The American Presidency

Landmark Objects

Conestoga Wagon

America **on the** Move

The First Ladies

American Stories

First Car, 1903

Do you know what POTUS stands for?

ANSWERS
First car driven across US—America on the Move;
George Washington's uniform—American Presidency;
Dorothy's ruby red slippers—American Stories;
Mary Lincoln's dress—The First Ladies;
Greensboro lunch counter—Landmark Objects

ANSWER
President of the United States

Photo Tip!

While visiting the American Presidency exhibit, stand behind the **POTUS** podium for your picture!

My favorite exhibit **at the** American History Museum:

National Air and Space Museum—
from early planes to moon rocks

The Smithsonian's Air and Space Museum has the largest collection of airplane and space history in the United States!

You can see exhibits and models that will teach you about the history of flying.

After you've explored sky and space, try to guess some of the museum's most famous artifacts!

Leonardo has given you some clues:

Hint #1

Two brothers worked for four years to design me. Though I am heavier than air, I flew 852 feet at Kitty Hawk, North Carolina. If you flew to DC on an airplane, you can thank me! What am I?

Hint #2

I am one of five of my kind on display in the museum. Though barely wider than your fingernail, I am a big deal! I traveled all the way from the moon so visitors like you could visit me in the Boeing Milestone of Flight Hall. What am I?

ANSWERS
1903 Wright Flyer; lunar (moon) rock

The National Archives— America's important papers

The United States of America was founded with two very important documents: the Declaration of Independence and the Constitution. You can see the original papers at The National Archives,* a beautiful building that honors these important pieces of history.

*archives: a place where historical papers are kept

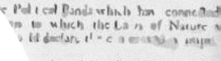

Did you know?

Two men who signed the Declaration of Independence, **Thomas Jefferson** (third president) and **John Adams** (second president) **both died** on July 4th, 1826 😢. That was the 50th anniversary of the Declaration of Independence.

Jacob Shallus, who was a printer or "engrosser," is the one whose penmanship appears on the Constitution. He had no part in coming up with the actual contents, but his handwriting is some of the most recognizable in American history. Look at the original document and the words below.
Can you write like Jacob?

We the People

Some **sad** history ... Ford's Theatre **and** the Petersen House

President Abraham Lincoln

Ford's Theatre has a famous place in history because of what happened there. And Leonardo will tell you all about it ...

Ford's Theatre was one of President Abraham Lincoln and his wife's favorite places. On April 14, 1865, they went there to see the play *Our American Cousin*. During the performance, Lincoln was shot by one of the actors—John Wilkes Booth 😮. President Lincoln was quickly rushed across the street to the Petersen boarding house, where he died the next morning.

Did you know?

Today, the president is protected by the Secret Service, but this special guard service did not start until 1901. When President Lincoln went to the theater, only his wife was with him.

Today, the theater honors President Lincoln by welcoming visitors like you who want to learn more about him and American history. It's also still a working theater, where people can see plays and musicals.

After you visit the theater, take a walk over to the Petersen House to see the room where the president died.

 Search for the following objects in the Petersen House bedroom. Then find them in the puzzle!

bed   paintings   dresser
chairs   book   candle

```
I P C J A A K B S N
A Z A H Y C O G B O
A H N H A O N D E B
X P D F K I V N X X
D U L C T S R T A D
Q E E N J S H S F N
U U I D Z Y Y W I L
A A J D R E S S E R
P A C G J C S Z J M
R A T G T W I K C U
```

Capitol Hill—
US Government in action

Capitol Hill is the term used to describe the area that includes the US Capitol Building, the Supreme Court, and the Library of Congress.

The Supreme Court

There are hundreds of courts in the United States, but the Supreme Court deals with the most important cases—and the cases lower courts don't agree on! Instead of just one judge, the **Supreme Court has nine** 😮. Each one votes in every case. If the Supreme Court is in session during your visit to DC, you may be able to step into the gallery and watch a case during trial.

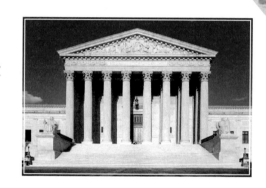

The Library of Congress

Did you know?

Supreme Court judges are chosen by the president, but they have to be approved by the US Senate. After a long questioning process, the Senate votes. Once they are voted in, judges serve on the Supreme Court for their entire lives!

Welcome to the largest—and oldest!—library in the United States! It is home to more than

- 883 miles of shelves
- 155 million **historical items**
- 33 million books (in 460 languages!)
- 68 million manuscripts
- 13.5 million photographs
- 6.5 million pieces of music
- more than 5 million maps
- and over 3.4 million recordings!
  WOW 😮...

33

US Capitol Building—
where the laws are made

The US Capitol Building is where members of Congress gather to make US laws. The US Congress is "bicameral," which means it has **two houses**: the Senate and the House of Representatives.

Each of the states elects two senators. There are **100 senators**.

The number of representatives each state can elect is based on the number of people who live in the state. There are 435 representatives.

Did you know?

A crypt (or burial vault) was built under the Capitol rotunda—but no one was ever buried there ... The tomb was made for George Washington. But when he died, his will asked that he be buried at Mount Vernon, his plantation.

When you visit the Capitol Building, Leonardo wants you to be sure to see the National Statuary Hall Collection. It's a beautiful circular room filled with statues donated by each of the 50 states. Since each state contributed two statues, there are over 100 figures of famous and important Americans.

Do you recognize any of them? Try to find the statues below and write their names and their states.

ANSWERS 1-Father Damien (Hawaii); 2-Helen Keller (Alabama); 3-Dwight D. Eisenhower (Kansas)

 1) _____

 2) _____

 3) _____

Martha Washington

President George Washington

Mount Vernon—
what was it like to live in the 1700s?

Even though you may be eager to tour the mansion and the grounds, take a few minutes to watch the video in the museum. You will learn facts about the life of Washington that are sure to make your experience more interesting.

You'll have to travel away from the National Mall and the city of Washington, DC, to visit Mount Vernon—George Washington's plantation home. Here, you'll learn about the life of the first president and his family, and you'll also get a firsthand look at what it was like to live in America in the 1700s.

☐ Be sure to walk through the mansion where Washington lived with his wife, Martha.
☐ Explore the stables.
☐ Visit the gardens.
☐ Check the blacksmith shop.
☐ Even visit Washington's tomb—where George and Martha are both buried.

Leonardo has put together some fun facts about Mount Vernon for you to keep in mind as you explore:

• The mansion's Banquet Hall was where George Washington received the news that he had been elected US President.
• Washington's favorite room was his library. When he died, his library held over 880 books! He considered the room his private retreat, and no one could enter it without an invitation from Washington.
• The beautiful gardens were designed by Washington himself after the Revolutionary War.

My favorite thing I learned at Mount Vernon: _____

DC games!

What am I?

Quizzes!

Can you guess which Washington, DC, site is being described?

1. I'm full of American treasures, including one president's top hat and another's military uniform. Visit me and sing along to the National Anthem as you gaze in awe at the Star-Spangled Banner.

_____

2. Come to me for a play, or to learn about the 16th President.

_____

3. Here, Senators and Representatives vote on whether or not a bill should become a law.

_____

Trivia!

1. Which **war did not** damage Washington, DC?

      a. Civil War   b. World War II   c. War of 1812

2. How **many memorial stones line the inside** of the Washington Monument?

      a. 193   b. 180   c. 93

3. Which **neighborhood is the oldest** in DC?

      a. Arlington   b. Foggy Bottom   c. Georgetown

ANSWERS Who Am I? 1. Museum of American History; 2. Ford's Theatre; 3. Capitol Building. Trivia Answers: 1. b., 2. a., 3. c.

A Washington, DC, word search

Can You Find These Words in the Puzzle?

Constitution
Monuments
President
Capitol
History
Congress
Smithsonian

~~Spangled~~
Banner
Supreme Court
Lincoln
Jefferson
White House

M W H S S J Q M W A P N
O D H L S O J N N R F O
N E K I T E S A E Z B I
U L E N T I R S Z A B T
M G J C U E I G N U R U
E N G O Z D H N N U K T
N A O L E D E O O O Y I
T P V N O R L C U S C T
S S T W N O E I D S T S
U A U Y T M Y X P I E N
M H L I E W A Q Y D Y O
R O P R M S E S B D U C
M A P I C Z D U I L L Z
C U S S R O O W G T H V
S M I T H S O N I A N M
H N O S R E F F E J G J
H I S T O R Y P B B Z Y

Can you break the code?

Use the key below to decode Leonardo's journal entry about his trip to Washington, DC!

Q = M   K = U   Z = O   X = E   J = I

I had a great time in WASHJNGTZN, DC (_ _ _ _ _ _ _ _ _ _, _ _)! I saw a lot of cool monuments, explored amazing museums, and got to visit George Washington's QZKNT VXRNZN (_ _ _ _ _ _ _ _ _ _ _)!

One of my favorite places to visit was the National Museum of Natural History, where I learned about all kinds of things like diamonds, primates, and DJNZSAKRS (_ _ _ _ _ _ _ _ _). There sure are a lot of interesting animals in the world!

At THX AJR and SPACX (_ _ _ _ _ _ and _ _ _ _ _) Museum, we saw lots of old airplanes and space shuttles, and I got to touch a lunar (moon) rock!

But my favorite part about Washington, DC, was THX LJNCZLN QXQZRJAL (_ _ _ _ _ _ _ _ _ _ _ _ _ _ _ _ _ _ _). Then again, I also loved walking around the NATJZNAL QALL (_ _ _ _ _ _ _ _ _ _ _ _) and seeing a play at FZRD'S THXATRX (_ _ _ _ _ _ _ _ _ _ _ _). I guess I loved XVXRYTHJNG (_ _ _ _ _ _ _ _ _ _) about wonderful Washington, DC!

Connect the Names of These Famous DC Sites

Ford's	Monument
Capitol	Vernon
Washington	House
Mount	Hill
National Museum of	Banner
Star-Spangled	Theatre
White	Natural History

Answers to Word Connect:

Ford's Theatre, Capitol Hill, Mount Vernon, National Museum of Natural History, Star-Spangled Banner, White House, Washington Monument

Coloring Page

The White House

Supreme Court

SUMMARY OF THE TRIP

We had great fun, what a pity it is over ...

Which places did you visit? _____

Whom did you meet...

Did you meet tourists from other countries? **yes / no**
If you did meet tourists, where did they come from?
(Name their nationalities): _____

Shopping and souvenirs...

What did you buy on the trip? _____

What did you want to buy, but ended up not buying?

_____

Experiences

What are the most memorable experiences of the trip?

_____

_____

_____

_____

_____

Record each family member's favorite places:

_____ : _____

_____ : _____

_____ : _____

_____ : _____

Grade the most beautiful places

and the best experience of the journey as a family:

First place -

Second place -

Third place -

And now, a difficult task—discuss it with your family and decide ...

What did you enjoy most on the trip?

My Washington, DC, journal

Date	What did we do?

My Washington, DC, journal

Date	What **did we do?**

ENJOY MORE FUN ADVENTURES WITH LEONARDO AND FlyingKids

ITALY

THAILAND

JAPAN

FRANCE

GERMANY

SPAIN

AUSTRALIA

CHINA

USA

SPECIAL EDITIONS

UNITED KINGDOM

KIDS' ACTIVITY BOOK SERIES

AGES 4-8

FOR FREE DOWNLOADS OF MORE ACTIVITIES, GO TO WWW.THEFLYINGKIDS.COM

81286340R00027

Made in the USA
Middletown, DE
22 July 2018